Making Christmas Count!

A Kid's Guide to Keeping the Season Sacred

Written by
Ted O'Neal

Illustrated by
R. W. Alley

ONE
CARING
PLACE

Abbey Press
St. Meinrad, IN 47577

This book is dedicated to R.W. Alley,
whose creative energies and talents
bring joy and wisdom to a child's world.

Text © 2006 Ted O'Neal
Illustrations © 2006 Saint Meinrad Archabbey
Published by One Caring Place
Abbey Press
St. Meinrad, Indiana 47577

Library of Congress Catalog Number
2006928523

ISBN 978-0-87029-401-3

Printed in the United States of America

A Message to Parents, Teachers, and Other Caring Adults

Kids, especially, don't need to be told that Christmas "counts." They are generally tuned in to the excitement and anticipation! And yet, children can be among the first to forget what it is about the season that really counts. Much of this may have to do with what our culture—and we ourselves—teach and practice.

And yet, we who are Christ-ians know that Christmas is no ordinary feast; celebrating the birth of our Savior is indeed cause for excitement and enthusiasm on a genuinely deeper level.

Obviously, we grown-ups also enjoy the "less sacred" aspects of the season: gift-giving, decorating, caroling, feasting at the table, reuniting with family and friends. But, upon reflection, we find that many of these caring and sharing moments truly are sacred in themselves and are—or can become—spiritual experiences.

Christmas, after all, is about the spirit of love: Love come down to reside with us and—more—to save us. This little illustrated book tries to communicate that central message to young people.

And so it is a message about making Christmas count in all its facets and flavors; it is a book about recognizing the deepest "reasons for the season."

Yes, every bit of Christmas counts...and helping children keep the season sacred is one of the best presents we adults can offer them! May this book lend a hand.

—*Ted O'Neal*

FOURTEEN Gazillion

It sounds like the biggest possible number there is…and it's how many years it seems like you've been waiting for Christmas. It's the longest time ever!

Did you know there were billions of years before the first Christmas, too? And then about 2,000 years ago, it finally happened: Jesus was born, and there has been a Christmas every year since!

There will be a Christmas this year, too. So how can you make it one of the best ones ever? How can you make sure every bit of Christmas counts?

THIRTEEN—an Unlucky Number?

Do you know the word "superstition"? A superstition is a belief or trust in something that's not necessarily true. Some people believe that the number 13 is unlucky, for instance. That's a superstition.

But would you feel unlucky if you had 13 presents waiting for you under the tree at Christmas? Or what if you had 13 inches of snow on Christmas Eve…and Santa made it to your house anyway?!

At Christmas, all of us have reasons to feel lucky, to feel blessed. What are some of the reasons you feel lucky and blessed?

TWELVE Days of Christmas

You probably know the song "The Twelve Days of Christmas." You know: "On the first day of Christmas, my true love gave to me…"? Well, the 12 days are really the 12 days after Christmas.

The 12 days begin with Christmas and end with the Epiphany. The Epiphany remembers the day the Three Wise Men came and gave gifts to Jesus. In some places, families give each other a small gift on every one of the 12 days as a way of continuing this celebration. Other families wait to open their Christmas gifts on Epiphany.

The gifts remind us that Christmas is about giving. It's about love.

ELEVEN Ideas for What to Give

Getting presents is nice, of course. But when we *give*, we really make Christmas count. And giving presents doesn't mean just giving neat toys or things that can be wrapped in pretty paper. Here are 11 other really nice things to give:

1. Draw a picture for Grandpa.
2. Help Mom or Dad bake cookies.
3. Donate money to help children whose families have very little.
4. Help your parents take cans of food to the food bank.
5. Visit a nursing home.
6. Sing in the church choir.
7. Send homemade Christmas cards to relatives far away.
8. Be nice to someone you may not like very much.
9. Give a big Christmas hug to your brother or sister or mom or dad.
10. Do the dishes after the Christmas dinner.
11. Say a prayer for someone who may not be having a merry Christmas, because of sickness or suffering.

TEN Minutes of "The Christmas Story"

A great way to make Christmas special is to read the Bible stories of the first Christmas from the Gospels. Maybe Mom or Dad will read them with you.

In the Gospel of Matthew, we read about Mary, "who will have a son, and will name him Jesus—he will save his people from their sins." In Mark and John's stories, we hear Jesus' cousin, John the Baptist, telling us: "The man who will come after me (Jesus) is much greater than I am."

St. Luke tells "The Christmas Story" as most of us know it: "And while they [Mary and Joseph] were in Bethlehem, the time came for Mary to have her baby. She gave birth to her first son, wrapped him in cloths and laid him in a manger for there was no room for them in the inn."

NINE O'Clock Is Bedtime

When it's "the night before Christmas," nine o'clock might be a good time to go to bed. But in many places, Christians stay up and go to church at midnight!

At church they sing, "Silent Night, Holy Night." And it is a holy night—a night of "heavenly peace," like we sing in the song.

"Peace" is another thing that makes Christmas "count" in everyone's heart. Jesus comes to bring peace and talks about peace all the time. He says, "Peace be with you." "My peace I give to you." His followers are people of peace. As you go to sleep each night, a prayer for peace in the world is a wonderful thing to say. It makes Christmas count every day!

EIGHT Tiny Reindeer

You probably know all about Santa's reindeer. There's Dasher and Dancer, Prancer and Vixen, and all the rest. And you probably know what their "job" is, too: To help deliver Christmas presents.

What "job" do we have at Christmas? What can we "deliver"? How about delivering things like…

- Understanding—if we don't get everything we want for Christmas.
- Patience—when Mom and Dad are too busy for us.
- Happiness that shows—because we know there is a deeper reason to celebrate Christmas in our hearts.

SEVEN Wonders of the World

Christmas is such a wonderful event; it's surprising that it is not one of the "Seven Wonders of the World." You may be reading about these "ancient wonders" in school. Or maybe your parents can tell you about them.

The Great Pyramids of Egypt are the only "wonder" that you can still see today. All the rest are gone—ruined. They didn't last.

But Christmas can last! Even when all the presents are old or broken, there's still a great "wonder" left. It's the wonder of what God gave—living with us, and living inside us, too, in our hearts!

THE SIXTH of December

On December 6th every year, we celebrate the Feast of St. Nicholas. The name "Santa Claus" itself came from this name. (Say "St. Nicholas" really fast three times and you will see!)

Nicholas was a bishop who lived long ago, but his story lives on. He is remembered because he was so kind and generous. He gave gifts to people secretly—he didn't even care if people knew that he gave the gift. Wow!

It's important to remember that St. Nicholas gave because he wanted to honor God, who gave us the gift of his son, Jesus, on Christmas.

"GIMME FIVE!"

The saying, "Gimme five!" isn't really a Christmas saying, but it is a friendly, happy way that some people greet each other.

At Christmastime we greet each other with sayings like "Merry Christmas!" and "Happy Holidays!" and "Happy New Year!"

It's the joy of the season that makes people say these happy words. And joy is one of the best gifts there ever was. There is always plenty to be joyful about, isn't there, when we know how blessed we are by God?

FOUR Gifts for the Baby Jesus

Shortly after Jesus was born, the Three Wise Men came from far away, and gave presents to him. "And they gave him gifts of gold, frankincense, and myrrh."

Those gifts may seem a bit odd or different to us today—all except the gold. But all of these things were precious gifts at that time, and helped show how important Jesus was.

The *fourth* gift they gave to Jesus, and the one we don't think about, was the most precious of all: They made a long, hard trip, just to worship and adore Jesus. We give God a great gift every time we adore him, too!

THREE Wise Men

Yes, the Three Wise Men came to "adore" Baby Jesus. They knew he was a baby who was different from all others. Even kings would kneel before this baby!

Today, we celebrate our faith by going to church, praying, reading the Bible, and following what Jesus came to teach us about love and peace.

At Christmastime, we celebrate what God has done for us. God gave us Jesus to teach us how to live. And God gave us Jesus to give us the gift of life forever. No wonder the Three Wise Men gave Jesus that gold!

TWO People, Mary and Joseph

When you look at the "crèche" or "Christmas manger" in your home or at your church, or in a painting, you always see Baby Jesus with his mom and dad there beside him.

Mary and Joseph were both very holy people. That means they did what God *wanted them to do*. Best of all, they wanted to do what God wanted them to do!

That's a part worth remembering: God likes it very much knowing that we *want* to do what he wants.

ONE Baby Jesus

Christmas begins with the birth of one little baby, one person, Jesus. But Christmas is really about all people and God's love for them.

At Christmastime, it seems like the world becomes one, big, happy family. So we celebrate Christmas by doing special things with our "smaller" family at home—and we join in the happy spirit of our "larger" family around the world.

We unite in love and celebration. And we sing the truth loud and clear, every year: "Joy to the World, the Lord has come!"

Ted O'Neal has written a number of Elf-help books for children and for grown-ups. He holds a master's degree in English from Indiana State University and worked for a religious publishing firm in Cincinnati for many years. He and his wife, a school guidance counselor, are the parents of three children, and reside in southern Indiana.

R. W. Alley is the illustrator for the popular Abbey Press adult series of Elf-help books, as well as an illustrator and writer of children's books. He lives in Barrington, Rhode Island, with his wife, daughter, and son.